History of Video Games

David Paris and
Stephanie Herweck Paris

Consultants

Timothy Rasinski, Ph.D.
Kent State University

Lori Oczkus, M.A.
Literacy Consultant

Publishing Credits

Rachelle Cracchiolo, M.S.Ed., *Publisher*
Conni Medina, M.A.Ed., *Managing Editor*
Dona Herweck Rice, *Series Developer*
Emily R. Smith, M.A.Ed., *Content Director*
Stephanie Bernard and Seth Rogers, *Editors*
Robin Erickson, *Multimedia Designer*

Image Credits: p.7 illustration by Timothy J. Bradley; p.9 Rick Tribble; p.10 Creative Commons File:Atari Pong arcade game cabinet.jpg by Rob Boudon used under CC BY 2.0; pp.10-11 INTERFOTO / Alamy; p.12 Majdyk/Dreamstime; p.13 Arturo Pardavila III/Flickr; p.14 Neil Godwin/GamesMaster Magazine via Getty Images; p.16 Robtek/Dreamstime.com; p.18 Georges Seguin (Okki)/Wikimedia Commons; p.21 taylorhatmaker/Flickr; pp.22, 30 Wikimedia Commons; p.23 Lux Igitur / Alamy; pp.28-29 Ubisoft via Getty Images; p.29 urbanbuzz / Alamy; p.30 screenshot from Wikimedia Commons; p.31 theodore liasi / Alamy; p.32 DigiBarn Computer Museum; p.36 GOIMAGES / Alamy; p.41 LIONEL BONAVENTURE/AFP/ Getty Images; all other images from iStock and/or Shutterstock.

Teacher Created Materials
5301 Oceanus Drive
Huntington Beach, CA 92649-1030
http://www.tcmpub.com

ISBN 978-1-4938-3594-2

Printed in China 51497

Table of Contents

Games Everywhere. 4
Early Games 6
Arcade Revolution 10
Consoles Take Over 14
How Home Computers Fit in the Game 22
Game Genres 24
Massively Multiplayer Online Gaming 32
Handhelds and Phones: Mobile Games 36
E-Sports 40
The Future of Games:
New Ideas and New Technology 42
Glossary. 44
Index 45
Check It Out! 46
Try It! 47
About the Authors 48

Games Everywhere

These days, video games seem to be almost everywhere. They are seamlessly integrated into our entertainment landscape. There are TV shows based on games, and there are games based on TV shows. There are movies based on games and games based on movies! If you carry a cell phone, you probably have video game apps on it. If you have a computer, there may be games on that, too. The industry estimates that 155 million Americans play video games and that there are about 1.2 billion **gamers** worldwide!

Interesting History

Of course, that was not always the case. Before the World Wide Web existed, the video games that were available looked very different from the ones you can get today. So, how long have computer and video games been around? How did they get started, and how did they become the global force they are today? That, gamers, is a very good story.

Some Gaming Stats

Global sales of video games are about $100 billion per year. The average game player is 35 years old. About 56 percent of gamers are male and 44 percent are female. And four out of five families in the United States own a device used to play video games.

Kids, Parents, and Gaming

About 59 percent of parents whose children play video games say they play also. And 63 percent say that video games are a positive part of their children's lives.

Fun—With Limits

Even if parents approve of their children playing games, they don't want them to spend every moment on gaming. About 79 percent of parents put time limits on their children's video game play.

Early Games

How far back can we trace computer gaming? Maybe further than you think. The first use of a computer to play games was an **electromechanical** Nim player shown at the 1940 World's Fair. Edward Condon, a distinguished nuclear physicist of the time, developed what he called the Nimatron.

The earliest games may seem simple now, but today's games were built on ideas from the ones that came before. The first creation that can properly be called a video game was *OXO*. It played Tic-Tac-Toe. Another early game was *Tennis for Two*. It used an **oscilloscope** to show the path of a tennis ball on a court. Players would click a button to hit the ball and use a knob to control the angle.

Spacewar! was built at the Massachusetts Institute of Technology in 1962. It was a two-player game where each player controlled a different spaceship. The ships shot at each other around the gravity well of a star. People thought it was so much fun that they made their own versions with new features such as mines and cloaking. *Spacewar!* inspired many future games.

Using What You Know

An oscilloscope is an instrument used to show changes in electrical waves over time. Physicist William Higinbotham knew and understood the oscilloscope, and so he used it when creating *Tennis for Two*.

What Is Nim?

Nim is an ancient mathematical strategy game in which players take turns removing playing pieces from piles. The players may remove as many pieces from any one pile as they like, as long as they remove at least one. The object is to force the other player to remove the final piece.

Artificial Intelligence

When tested against humans, the Nimatron machine won 9 out of 10 games.

Nimatron

The Advent of Commercial Games

Large companies, universities, or science institutions owned all the earliest games. But in the early 1970s, games were being made for regular people to buy. Games were going commercial!

The first commercially sold coin-operated video game, or **cabinet**, arrived in 1971. It was called *Computer Space*. Nolan Bushnell and Ted Dabney created it. Players flew a spaceship and battled flying saucers. If a player could outperform the saucers for 90 seconds, the game would give another 90 seconds of game-play.

The Earliest Console

In 1968, the electronics company Magnavox started exploring a new idea. They wanted to make a machine on which a person could play multiple games at home. By 1972, they were ready to release the very first **video game console**. It was made to connect to a TV. They called it *The Odyssey*. By modern standards, it was very clunky. It had removable **circuit boards** called "game cards." A player could swap them in and out to change the games. It also came with dice, fake money, and playing cards. The creators wanted to make the console feel familiar to people who were used to board games.

Coin-Operated Video Games

In September 1971, Stanford University installed a game called *Galaxy Game* in its Student Union. It was not available commercially, but people at Stanford could play the game. Players would get one game for a dime and three games for a quarter.

THINK LINK

As you read through this book, keep these questions in mind:

- How did each new game build off the ones that came before it?
- How did the different kinds of gaming **platforms** affect the development of the others?
- How did the evolving technology affect the kinds of games that were being made?

Odyssey²

Arcade Revolution

The first successful video game company was Atari. It was started in June 1972 by Nolan Bushnell and Ted Dabney. The very first engineer they hired was Allan Alcorn. He designed *Pong* as an in-house test. He based it on the ping-pong style game from The Odyssey. But *Pong* was so much fun that Atari decided to sell it as its first major product! It became the first commercially successful coin-operated video game. Many more games were soon to follow.

Some Deals Don't Work Out

Magnavox made a deal with Atari when Atari used the *Pong* idea. Magnavox was supposed to receive a percentage of the money from games Atari released that year. But Atari did not release their games during the time period that mattered. Magnavox lost out!

A Big Hit

Pong is a two-person, tennis-like game. Each player controls a paddle, which can be moved up and down on the screen. A **pixelated** ball bounces back and forth between the players and bounces off the paddles.

Pong

A Sneaky Competitor

Distributors are companies that make sure products get where customers can buy them. When the first video games were being made, each distributor insisted on being the only one a company worked with. If Atari worked with the distributor that put games at ice cream parlors, for instance, Atari couldn't work with the one that put games in pizza parlors. Atari got sneaky. Bushnell, the company's cofounder, convinced his long-time friend Joe Keenan to start a new company. He called it Kee Games. Kee Games made almost the same games as Atari, but it used different distributors. That way, the same games would be played in twice as many places!

Arcades Flourish

Throughout the late 1970s and early 1980s, **arcade** games broke new barriers. Atari and Kee Games soon had many competitors. By the mid-1980s, there were at least 15 companies making arcade video games. Most were in the United States and Japan.

In 1978, the Japanese company Taito released one of the most popular titles of all time. *Space Invaders* showed rows of aliens moving toward Earth. The player moved a laser cannon at the bottom of the screen. The goal was to shoot the aliens before they hit the ground.

In 1979, Atari released *Asteroids*. It sold over 70,000 arcade cabinets. That was a lot back then. But it was tiny compared with what came next.

In 1980, Namco put out the most successful arcade game of all time. It featured an iconic yellow character named Pac-Man. He ate dots while moving through a maze away from ghosts. This was a new kind of game, and it paid off. *Pac-Man* sold over 350,000 cabinets and made more than $2 billion!

Puck Man

Before releasing *Pac-Man* in North America, Namco released a different version of the same game in Japan. It was called *Puck Man*. But Japanese gamers were more interested in shooting games like *Asteroids*. So, Namco was surprised when *Pac-Man* became a super-hit.

The Golden Age

The 1970s and early 1980s were a great time for video games. This time was called the Golden Age. The top arcade cabinets brought in an average of $400 each per week. Popular games were *Donkey Kong*, *Frogger*, *Galaxian*, *Tron*, *Dig-Dug*, and *Centipede*. It is estimated that there were about 13,000 arcades across America at that time!

Consoles Take Over

Consoles have been around almost as long as commercial games have. But originally, consoles didn't have a lot of users. It was convenient to have a console in your home, but they were expensive and there were not very many games to play. Plus, companies didn't know how to market them. Should they try to sell them to kids? Kids didn't really have enough money to buy the consoles on their own. Would older people buy them? Companies didn't know. A lot of people who enjoyed video games thought it was easier and more fun to go to an arcade. They could hang out with their friends, and it only cost a quarter to play each game.

But every year the technology got better, and every year, more and more people started playing games. In 1985 and 1986, a new generation of consoles hit the market. The Nintendo Entertainment System (NES) and Sega's Master System helped change the focus of gaming. Suddenly, arcades were regarded as less important. Home gaming systems were seen as the promise of the future.

Tetris

In 1984, a Russian video game took the world by storm. Up until that time, almost all the popular games had come out of Japan or the United States. *Tetris* is a tile matching game with very simple mechanics. It spawned the popularity of the puzzle game **genre**.

Seal of Approval

Unlike Atari, both Nintendo and Sega required game developers to submit their games for approval before they could be sold in stores as an official game for their consoles. Approved games were given a seal that showed customers that the games met each company's strict quality standards.

The Console Wars

In 1989, things really started to heat up for the console world. Sega introduced its first 16-bit console, the Genesis. This was shortly followed by Nintendo's 16-bit Super NES (SNES). The "16-bit" part means that these systems had vastly improved graphics from earlier systems. For gamers, it was great! There were so many games to choose from, and since the competition between systems was fierce, prices stayed relatively low. But for the gaming companies, it was more stressful. Each one wanted to have the best-selling systems and the best-selling games. The media called this time period "The Console Wars." Who won? In this first battle between the Genesis and the SNES, Nintendo came out ahead but only by a little. Sega sold $40 million worth of Genesis machines worldwide. But SNES boasted a larger number of popular game titles. In particular, gamers were drawn to *The Legend of Zelda: A Link to the Past* and *Donkey Kong Country*.

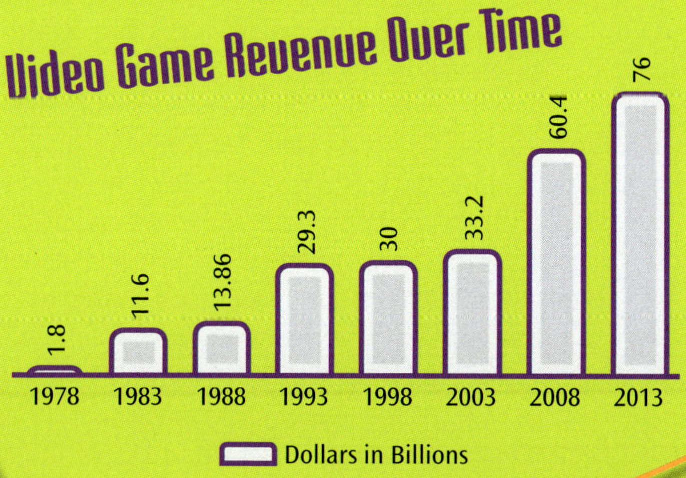

STOP! THINK...

The chart above shows how much money was made by the worldwide video game industry since 1978. Use the chart to answer these questions.

- What year would be the next expected bar on the graph?
- Predict how much money you would expect the industry to earn that year. Why?
- There are several points on the graph where the revenue grows very rapidly. What factors might explain that kind of growth?

The Console Wars Continue

As time passed, gaming systems got better and better. The graphics and sounds became richer and more beautiful. The games got more involved. They had deeper story lines and more innovative game play. Still, the console makers had a problem. Unlike the early days of video games, most everyone now had a **home computer**. Why buy a special system for games when your computer could play most of them? Consoles cost between $250 and $500. Each game cost between $20 and $80. There were fewer people willing or able to spend that kind of money for games.

Mortal Kombat 3 arcade cabinet

Still Winners?

Two new types of games gave dying arcades new hope. One-on-one fighting games and dancing games were more fun to play in groups and against new opponents. Games such as *Mortal Kombat* and *Dance-Dance Revolution* brought customers back to arcades.

Even if a family chose to buy a console system, how could each company convince them to buy *their* machine? During the late 1990s and early 2000s, console makers each tried to find something special they could do that no one else could copy. Some companies made new remote controllers that had motion sensors. Others made efforts to give more value for the money. For instance, some consoles let owners play DVDs and Blu-Ray Discs on the machines.

Top Five

Over the years, it has become more common to find video game consoles in people's homes. These five systems have sold more than any of their competitors.

1. PlayStation 2 (2000)—155 million sold
2. Nintendo DS (2004)—153.98 million sold
3. GameBoy (1989)—118.69 million sold
4. PlayStation (1994)—102.5 million sold
5. Wii (2006)—100.9 million sold

DIG DEEPER!

The Mystery of the Buried Extra-Terrestrial

1982: Atari makes a very unpopular game. ***E.T. The Extra-Terrestrial*** is based on the movie of the same name. Many critics call it one of the worst video games of all time. The game's graphics are weak, and it isn't very entertaining. Some estimates say there are millions of unsold copies!

1980 1987 1994

1984: Financially troubled Atari is sold and its top officers fired. Information about the possible burial becomes difficult to get.

1983: Rumors start that Atari has secretly sent between 10 and 20 semi-trailer trucks filled with ***E.T. The Extra-Terrestrial*** and several other games and unsold consoles to a New Mexico landfill. Rumors increase when concrete is inexplicably poured over the site.

2004: Rumors continue. Many people, including the chief programmer for ***E.T.***, officially state that the whole thing is just an **urban legend**. Others insist that there are 3.5 million games buried at the site.

2013: A Canadian film crew gets permission to **excavate** the site as part of a **documentary** on the story.

2001 2008 2015

2014: On April 26, the site is opened. Remnants of ***E.T.*** and other games are found! The manager originally in charge of the burial is present. He admits that the company buried 728,000 cartridges. About 1,300 of them are retrieved before the site is reburied.

How Home Computers Fit in the Game

When the first video games were made, most people had never come in contact with a computer. Certainly, no one had their own personal computers in their homes. But with the advent of home computing in the 1980s, suddenly computers were everywhere. Many people were still not very comfortable with them, though. What could computer manufacturers do to make computers more fun and accessible? They could include games! Games and home computers have gone together since the beginning. The Apple II was one of the first widely sold home computers. And it had hundreds of game titles from which to choose.

Solitaire and Minesweeper

When personal computers first came out, people didn't know how to use a mouse. *Solitaire* was pre-loaded to teach people to drag and drop the cards. *Minesweeper* was included to teach how to right and left click!

Back and Forth

As computers became more and more powerful, the games made for them became more advanced. But home computers are meant to do things other than just play games. Because of that, they can't always match the experience of consoles. In practical terms, though, what matters is the economy. When the economy is good, people tend to buy consoles. This is because they usually have extra money to spend on entertainment. When the economy is bad, people stick to computer games.

Video Games Spawn Physical Games

The very successful ***Warcraft*** video games inspired tabletop games. There are also novels, collectible card games, comic books, and manga. There is even a movie based on the games!

Game Genres

Genres are loose classifications that group similar games. Some games fit into many genres. Others don't really seem to fit into any existing genre at all. As new games are built, new genres are developed. So, what are some general genres for video games, and when did they come about? Let's take a brief tour.

Role-Playing Games

In the 1970s, *Dungeons & Dragons* (D&D) made headlines with its new style of pen-and-paper gaming. It also influenced computer-game design. D&D led to an entire genre of games known as **role-playing games** (RPGs). In RPGs, the player creates one or more characters. Each character has its own identity, story, and attributes. As the games progress, these characters grow and change, becoming more powerful over time.

Ultima is a good example of a fantasy RPG. It offers a fantastic world to explore. This style of gaming has evolved over the years. Originally, the style relied primarily on traditional fantasy worlds, much like those created by Lord of the Rings author J. R. R. Tolkien. But now, it includes environments of all sorts. People can play the parts of space explorers, magical creatures, athletes, mobsters, missionaries, or almost anything else that can be dreamed up.

Physical Games Become Video Games

As with any art form, game developers get inspired by other media. *Magic: The Gathering* is a very popular collectible card game that now has online versions. And the pen-and-paper game D&D continues to inspire online RPGs.

Final Fantasy

When consumers like a game, developers try to make more games like it. Often this leads to copycats, but it also leads to long-running series. One of the most successful RPG series is Final Fantasy. The series was popular from the beginning in Japan but really took off in the United States with *Final Fantasy VII*.

Polyhedral dice are commonly used to play D&D and other pen-and-paper games.

Platformers

In early games, players did simple movements to avoid hazards. Adding a single action button could advance some of these movements. The action button was often used as a jump command. This combination of moving and jumping gave birth to a genre known as the *platformer*. In this genre, players try to reach a goal by bouncing and weaving through mazes filled with hazards and enemies. The genre is named after the platforms that characters climb in the games.

As time went on, games added their own specialties. For example, *Metroid* introduced the idea of unlocking special items to let players go back to revisit areas. *Sonic the Hedgehog* shows us how much fun it is to blast along with crazy speed.

Mario, Video Game Superstar

One of the platformer genre's lasting stars is Mario. He made his first appearance in ***Donkey Kong*** (1981) and has been seen in many groundbreaking titles over the years. He can also be found on everything from television shows to comic books to shampoo bottles!

Strategy

Strategy gaming is a huge category with many sub-genres. In strategy games, players make tactical and strategic decisions. The goal is to gain advantage of the other player over time. The earliest strategy video games were digital versions of board games, such as chess, where each player took one turn at a time.

But this genre has changed a lot over time. For instance, one sub-genre is called the 4X strategy game. This stands for "expand, explore, exploit, and exterminate." Stronger computers meant there was no reason that turns needed to happen one at a time. **Real-time strategy games** emerged, and the game world began to feel more like a living thing.

Historic Historical Strategy

Eastern Front was a ground-breaking early strategy title. It was based on World War II. The game used scenarios that mimicked the Russian and German battles of that time. It featured a computer **artificial intelligence** (AI) opponent as well as other new ideas.

Adventure

Adventure games tell stories. Early titles such as *King's Quest* and *Legend of Zelda* gave players huge worlds to explore as the stories unfolded. There were usually set sequences of events, which led players from one challenge to the next.

In 1993, a new type of adventure game was introduced. In games such as *Myst*, players are not shown the story directly. Instead, they explore relatively unguided. Players determine the story for themselves. Players don't necessarily "win." But once they uncover most of the puzzles and mysteries, they unlock fun, end-game animations.

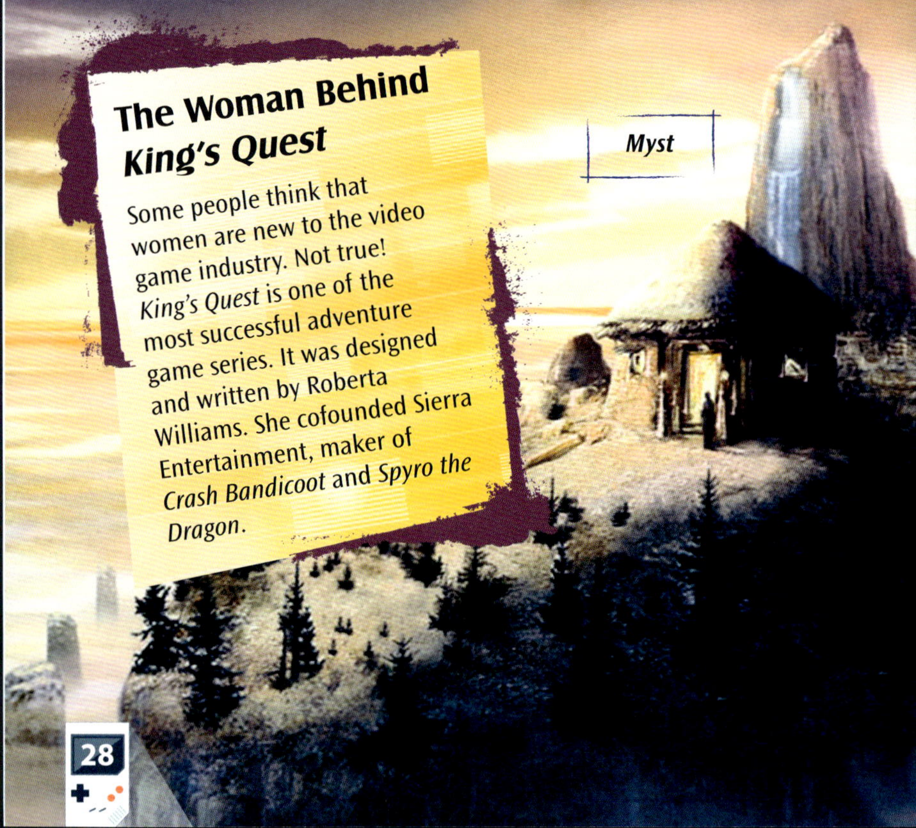

Myst

The Woman Behind *King's Quest*

Some people think that women are new to the video game industry. Not true! *King's Quest* is one of the most successful adventure game series. It was designed and written by Roberta Williams. She cofounded Sierra Entertainment, maker of *Crash Bandicoot* and *Spyro the Dragon*.

Sports Games Bring in New Players

Whatever your sport of choice, there is probably a video game out there based on it. Game makers like creating sports games because each sport comes with its own fans (who are likely to buy the game)!

Action

Action games focus on reflexes and quick choices. These games challenge players to respond correctly in an instant. Action has many sub-genres. These include sports, fighting, and action-adventure games.

Side-view fighting games were around by 1984. They are called side-view games because the characters are seen from the side to show the punches and kicks. *Karate Champ* defined much of this sub-genre early on. Two players battle with kicks and punches. The challenge is timing and position.

Sports games are a kind of action game. They make the players feel as if they are playing real-world sports. They often include celebrities that most gamers will recognize. ***Madden NFL***, for example, has full rosters of known teams for the player to interact with and play as.

Simulation

Simulation games let players live out real-life scenarios in video games. The first really famous simulation game was *SimCity*. It was first created in 1989. Players were able to build cities. They could tinker with and observe many parts of planning a city or world. All sorts of other simulations followed. Players could play with everything from the evolution of life to the control of a single anthill.

In 2000, *The Sims* burst onto the scene. This game demonstrated how much fun it was to simulate the lives of ordinary (or extraordinary) people. Players could set up homes and relationships. They could watch Sims try to live their lives as players nudged them with their wishes.

Educational Games

Educational games can be considered a genre of their own. But really, most of these games also fit into other genres. Math games are often puzzles or quiz games. *Oregon Trail* is an educational adventure game. There are educational action games and RPGs, as well.

screenshot from *Oregon Trail*

A simple yet immensely powerful game called *Minecraft* came along in 2008. The basic graphics were quite boxy and dated. But *Minecraft* included a powerful building capability. This allowed players to build their own world. They could make anything they wanted based on real life or fantasy. The program acts like a set of creative tools.

Gaming to Learn

Gaming challenges are increasingly difficult, and games capture our imaginations. More and more educators use games to help students learn everything from history to computer coding. There are even special websites where teachers can trade *Minecraft* lesson ideas!

Massively Multiplayer Online Gaming

Massively Multiplayer Online games (MMOs) let many people play at the same time. The first many-player game was called *Maze War*. It was made in 1974. It wasn't really "online," though. It needed cables to attach different machines.

After that time, every new step in technology led to new MMOs. *Zork* was released in 1977 and was followed by Essex **Multi-User Dungeon** (MUD) in 1978.

Text-based MUDs became popular on college campuses. They were similar to modern online RPGs but with one big difference. There were no pictures at all. A running column of words told you what was going on in the game. At this point, though, no one had figured out how to earn money from MMOs.

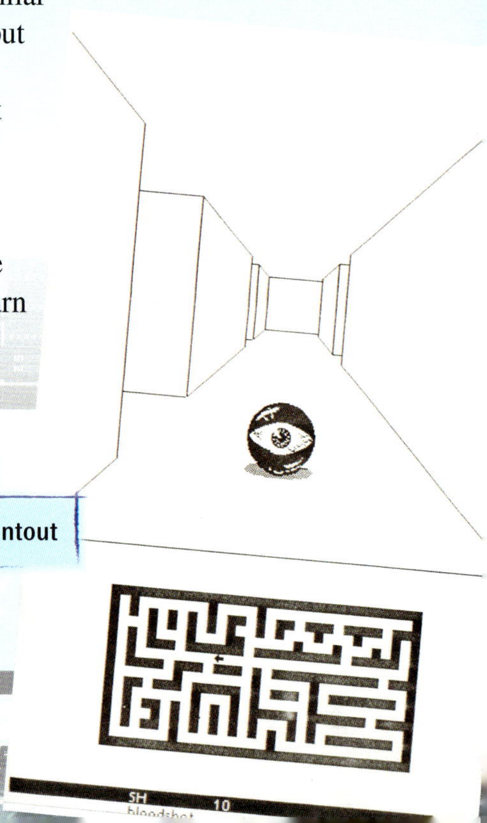

Maze War printout

Graphical MMOs

At first, no one had the computing power to coordinate graphics among many players at once. In 1996, *Meridian 59* became the first commercial **Massively Multiplayer Online Role-Playing Game** (MMORPG). The first known Internet-based, subscription-funded MMORPG was *Valhalla*. It was a text-based MUD started by David Paris in 1990. The game boasted complex skills, magic, classes, items, and interactive AI. Many of these elements live on in today's MMORPGs.

```
You have entered a large throne
room. A glittering crown sits on a
shelf.

:look at crown

The crown is glittery. You could
probably wear it.

:take crown

You take the crown.

:wear crown

You put the crown onto your head.
POOF! You have turned into a frog
prince!

:look at self

You are quite dashing for an
amphibian. Nice crown!
```

text-based game scroll

Wow! WoW

In 2004, Blizzard Entertainment released the most defining and dominant MMO to date: *World of Warcraft* (WoW). The creators did not focus on new features. Instead, they concentrated on doing basic things very well. They also targeted a very broad group of potential players. They wanted kids and adults of all backgrounds to be interested in the game. And they held to extremely high production standards. That means there were not many bugs, the game was easy to learn, and the graphics were beautiful, but the game could still be played on an average computer.

The results were wildly popular. The game boasted 12 million active subscriptions at its peak! WoW was so successful for so long that many other game makers stopped trying to compete with it. In some ways, it was nearly impossible for them to compete. New games had to spend a lot of money up front, and even then, their virtual worlds were small in comparison.

An MMO world with more content to explore has an advantage. Players want to be able to immerse themselves in the world. They want to explore and find new challenges. WoW has been actively doing this for over 10 years. It adds new in-game locations and challenges all the time.

World of Warcraft

That Takes a Lot of Resources

- At its height, Blizzard had 20,000 computer servers around the globe hosting WoW.
- It took 68 engineers to manage all that hardware.
- Blizzard had data centers in 10 locations: Washington, California, Texas, Massachusetts, France, Germany, Sweden, South Korea, China, and Taiwan.

Changing Times

New genres of games are becoming more popular. In November 2015, *World of Warcraft* subscriptions were down to about 5.6 million. But that is still a number any other MMO would be happy to have!

Handhelds and Phones: Mobile Games

Just as with other game platforms, there were early versions of handheld game devices. The first one was in 1976, titled *Auto Race*. You may notice, the title sounds like the name of one game. That is exactly what it was. Early handhelds contained only single games.

In 1989, Nintendo produced the GameBoy. It was capable of playing a wide range of games by using plug-in cartridges. The GameBoy and later handheld gaming systems were more limited than their larger home console cousins. But handhelds allowed the user to play games anywhere easily and conveniently. Their low prices and portability made them especially fitting for younger players.

Pokémon

Pokémon was developed for the GameBoy in Japan and first released in 1996. *Pokémon* is short for the Japanese title, "Pocket Monsters." The game introduced virtual pet-raising. And it was coupled with a powerful collection system. Like other popular games, *Pokémon* inspired television shows, films, a trading card game, manga, and soundtracks. *Pokémon* is so popular that it still continues to release new titles.

Even the Big Guys Make Mistakes

During the 1990s, Apple wanted to keep tight control over what features went on their home computers. They made it very difficult for game developers to create games that would work on Apple machines. This meant that consumers who might want to play games were less likely to buy Apple computers. So, when they launched their iPhones and iPads, Apple made sure there would be plenty of games and apps available.

In the late 1990s, cell phones were getting more powerful. They had enough spare computing power that they too could be used to play simple games. As phones advanced, better and better games became available. First, they matched the earliest handheld titles such as *Snake* or *Tetris*. Then, they grew into a whole new market of games built expressly for phones. Games such as *Angry Birds* and *Words with Friends* became big hits.

The limited screen space means that only certain styles of games work well. Mobile games generally need to have simple, clear graphics and an easy ability to pause.

In Control

Gamers are sometimes as excited by the mechanisms of game control as they are about the games themselves! (Well, maybe not *as* excited, but close.) The controller is a device used to move and manipulate objects and characters in the game. It becomes an extension of the player, allowing him or her to "step inside" the game and play.

There are many different types of controllers, often depending on what the controller is supposed to do. Here are some of them. Who knows what's next in their **evolution**?

Ouch!

Controllers have evolved to support comfort for the player as well as ease of use. Since players often repeat motions over long periods of time, cramping or serious injury to the hands and wrists can occur. If players can't play, developers can't sell. Everyone wins with pain-free controllers!

Gamepad

This device is usually held in both hands and is operated by the player's thumbs and fingers. Buttons and toggles allow the player to move characters and objects.

Joystick

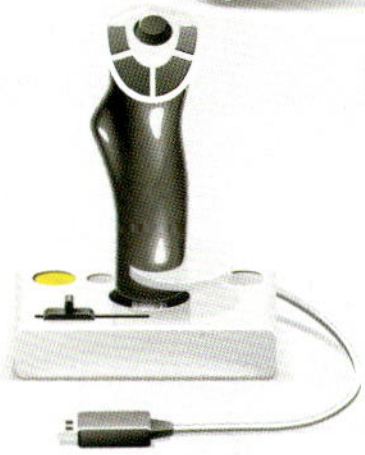

The player holds this device in the hand and toggles the stick to operate the game.

Trackball

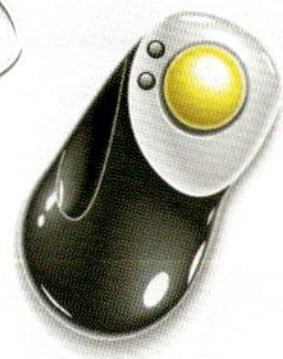

This controller is something like an upside-down mouse. It can be rolled to control the character or object.

Keyboard and Mouse

These are used to operate most computer games. A mouse allows the player to target direction easily and quickly.

Motion Sensor

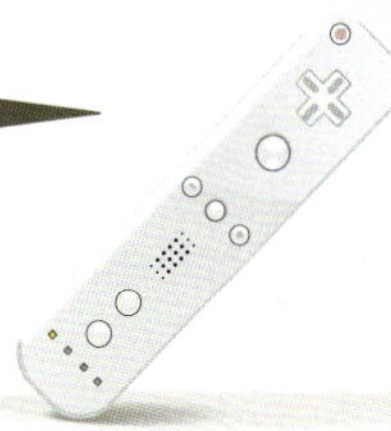

Sensor devices are sometimes used as virtual extensions of the player's body. The sensors can be directed to move items in the game. Sometimes, the item is an avatar of the player.

Touchscreen

Players can touch or swipe the screen of a computer or handheld system to target their movements.

E-Sports

Since the beginning of multiplayer gaming, people have competed against one another. There have even been people gathered to watch others compete. In 1980, Atari hosted a *Space Invaders* tournament. More than 10,000 players attended! Many similar one-time events have been held. But it wasn't until 1997 that the first professional gaming league got started.

Early pro gaming focused mostly on first-person action games. But there were sports games and fighting games, too. Then *Starcraft* was released. This was a highly competitive, real-time strategy game. It proved to be an outstanding game for pro competition. This was especially true in South Korea. South Koreans had embraced **e-sports** more quickly than the rest of the world. In South Korea, families might watch a football game on TV. Or they might choose to watch a *Starcraft* match.

It took a little longer for e-sports to be accepted in other places. The Multiplayer Online Battle Arena (MOBA) genre seems to be breaking the barrier. Titles such as *League of Legends* and *Defense of the Ancients* have brought professional gaming to the United States. Prize pools can reach as high as $10 million for a single tournament. A total of over 32 million viewers may tune in for a single event. E-sports seem to have arrived in a big way!

Top E-Sports

Game	Prize Pool for Top Tournament	Most People Watching at Once
League of Legends	$2.1 million	11 million
Defense of the Ancients II	$17 million	4.5 million
Counter Strike Global Offensive	$250,000	1 million
Smite	$2.6 million	estimated 2.9 million
World of Tanks	$300,000	120,000
Hearthstone	$250,000	estimated 250,000

video game tournament held in Paris, France, in May 2014

Cheating in E-sports

Just as with other competitive sports, there have been scandals in e-sports about drug use. Some competitors have used drugs to improve their performances and alertness. Organizers struggle with the problem. The Electronic Sports League has made the use of performance-enhancing drugs grounds for expulsion from competition.

The Future of Games: New Ideas and New Technology

We've learned the history of video games. But what is their future? Video games have come a long way from where they began. With the latest technology, not only can we carry our games around with us wherever we go, but we can also play games with people who live across the entire globe! It is hard to predict what will come next, but we can look at technology that is being developed and consider how it might be used. As computing power increases, so does our ability to create imaginary worlds. Many groups are working to create true "**virtual reality**" (VR). VR games would let people interact in **immersive** 3-D environments. There are even plans to make VR worlds that we can physically interact with through touch and smell!

With every new step in technology, new games spring up to feature the technology. But what happens when people have an idea for a cool new game that uses technology that doesn't exist yet? Well, that becomes an **impetus** for moving that technology forward!

The history of video games is less than 100 years old. But there is no doubt that the story will continue. Maybe you will claim a chapter for yourself!

Games Spur Innovations

Gamers push the limits of technology. To better compete, they want the most powerful machines with the fastest processors. They want the best graphics and the best sound, too. Computer makers listen! They work to make computers that gamers want to buy.

Do You Have an Idea?

What game would you love to play that you haven't seen available yet? Many video developers get their starts because they want to make games that they would like to play.

Glossary

arcade—location with many coin-operated games

artificial intelligence—the power for a computer to imitate human intelligence

cabinet—large coin-operated game in an arcade

circuit boards—rigid cards on which electronic circuits are printed or attached

distributors—companies that get a product out to where people can buy it

documentary—a movie or television show based on facts about real events and real people

e-sports—electronic sports; competitive gaming tournaments

electromechanical—related to the process of running on electricity

evolution—the process of change

gamers—people who play video games

genres—general ways of categorizing items

home computer—a computer small and inexpensive enough to be used in people's homes

immersive—creating a 3-D image that seems to surround the user

impetus—a force causing an activity to be done

Massively Multiplayer Online games—games that allow many people to play at once online

Massively Multiplayer Online Role-Playing game—a game in which many players create imaginary characters to interact with each other

Multi-User Dungeon—an early form of multiplayer game

oscilloscope—a device used in physics to measure energy over time

pixelated—individual digital pixels (dots) are able to be seen

platforms—systems that are used to play video games

real-time strategy games—strategy games that use time pressure to force players to make decisions

role-playing games—games in which players create characters with which to interact

side-view fighting games—games where characters are seen from the side to show punches or kicks

urban legend—a story based on hearsay that many people believe is true but is not

video game console—a dedicated machine that can play multiple games; usually used in homes

virtual reality—a representation of a believable environment that is not the one in which a person is currently situated

Index

action games, 29–30, 40
adventure games, 28–29
Alcorn, Allan, 10
Angry Birds, 37
Apple, 22, 37
arcade, 12–14, 18
Asteroids, 12
Atari, 10–12, 15, 20, 40
Auto Race, 36
Blizzard Entertainment, 34
Bushnell, Nolan, 8, 10
Centipede, 13
Computer Space, 8
Condon, Edward, 6
console, 8, 14–16, 18–20, 23, 36
Crash Bandicoot, 28
Dabney, Ted, 8, 10
Dance-Dance Revolution, 18
Defense of the Ancients (DotA), 40–41
Dig-Dug, 13
Donkey Kong, 13, 26
Donkey Kong Country, 16
Dungeons & Dragons, 24–25
E.T. The Extra-Terrestrial, 20–21
Eastern Front, 27
Final Fantasy, 25
Frogger, 13
Galaxian, 13
Galaxy Game, 8
GameBoy, 19, 36–37
GameBoy Advance, 19
Genesis, 16
genre, 15, 24, 26–27, 29–30
Golden Age, 13
handhelds, 36–37, 39
Higinbotham, William, 6
Karate Champ, 29
Kee Games, 11–12
King's Quest, 28
League of Legends, 40–41
Legend of Zelda, 16, 28
Madden NFL, 29
Magic: The Gathering, 25
Magnavox, 8, 10
Mario, 26
Massachusetts Institute of Technology, 6
Massively Multiplayer Online games (MMO), 32–35
Master System, 14
Mazewar, 32
Meridian 59, 33
Metroid, 26
Minecraft, 31
Minesweeper, 22
Mortal Kombat, 18
Myst, 28
Multiplayer Online Battle Arena (MOBA), 40
Namco, 12
Nimatron, 6–7
Nintendo, 14–16, 19, 36
Nintendo Entertainment System (NES), 14, 19
Odyssey, The, 8, 10
Oregon Trail, 30
OXO, 6
Pac-Man, 12
Paris, David, 33
platformer, 26
PlayStation, 19
Pokémon, 37
Pong, 10–11
Puck Man, 12
real-time strategy, 27, 40
role-playing games, 24
Sega, 14–16
SimCity, 30
Sims, The, 30
simulation, 30
Snake, 37
Solitaire, 22
Sonic the Hedgehog, 26
Space Invaders, 12, 40
Spacewar!, 6
sports games, 29, 40
Stanford University, 8
Starcraft, 40
strategy, 7, 27, 40
Super NES (SNES), 16
Taito, 12
Tennis for Two, 6
Tetris, 15, 37
Tolkien, J. R. R., 24
Tron, 13
Ultima, 24
Valhalla, 33
virtual reality (VR), 42
Warcraft, 23
Wii, 19
Williams, Roberta, 28
Words with Friends, 37
World of Warcraft (*WoW*), 34–35
Xbox 360, 19
Zork, 32

Check It Out!

Books

Alpert, Mark. 2015. *The Six*. Sourcebooks.

Card, Orson Scott. 1977. *Ender's Game*. Tom Doherty Associates.

Dashner, James. 2013. *The Eye of Minds*. Random House Children's Books.

Donovan, Tristan. 2010. *Replay: The History of Video Games*. Yellow Ant Media Ltd.

Videos

MGM. 2008. *WarGames*.

Websites

M&P Amusement. *Evolution of Arcade Games*. http://www.mpamusement.com/evolution-of-arcade-games.asp.

MMOs.com. http://mmos.com/.

PBS.org. *Video Game Revolution: History of Gaming*. http://www.pbs.org/kcts/videogamerevolution/history/.

The Richest. *10 Most Popular Consoles of All Time*. http://www.therichest.com/rich-list/most-popular/10-most-popular-game-consoles-of-all-time/.

The Strong, National Museum of Play. *Video Game History Timeline*. http://www.museumofplay.org/icheg-game-history/timeline/.

Try It!

You've just been offered a job as a major video game creator to come up with a brand-new, exciting video game. What type of world would you create? How can you make this game the best one yet? You've got some decisions to make:

- Draw a picture or write a description of the characters that will be featured in your video game.
- Decide what kind of special features your game has.
- Decide what the end goal of the game will be.
- Plan some of the things someone will need to play the game (a console, a mobile device, etc.).
- Think about the world or place in which your video game is set. Is it the normal, everyday world? Is it a mystical land or galaxy?

About the Authors

David Paris is a game producer/programmer/designer who has loved games since he was very young. He originally did mainstream application and operating system work, while building games on the side. Eventually, he realized that it was better to just do what he loves and now makes games full time.

Stephanie Herweck Paris is a writer, a mom, an educator, and a gamer. She especially enjoys RPGs, strategy games, puzzlers, and adventure games. When she isn't writing, teaching, or gaming, she can be found exploring real-life castles with her family and friends.